BLAST OFF!
PLUTO
AND OTHER DWARF PLANETS

Helen and David Orme

ticktock

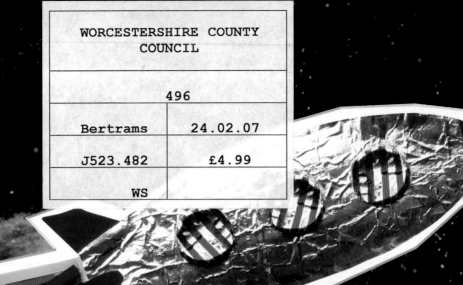

Copyright © ticktock Entertainment Ltd 2007
First published in Great Britain in 2006 by ticktock Media Ltd.,
Unit 2, Orchard Business Centre, North Farm Road,
Tunbridge Wells, Kent, TN2 3XF

ticktock project editor: Julia Adams
ticktock project designer: Emma Randall

We would like to thank: Sandra Voss, Tim Bones, James Powell,
Indexing Specialists (UK) Ltd.

ISBN 978 1 84696 056 7
Printed in China
A CIP catalogue record for this book is available from the British Library.

Picture credits
t=top, b=bottom, c=centre, l-left, r=right, bg=background
Hubble Space Telescope: 20; Mary Evans: 19b; NASA: 1tl, 7t, 8 (all, 12 (original), 22, 23 (all); Science Photo Library: front cover,
1br, 4/5bg (original), 6 (original), 7b, 9t (original), 9b, 11tl, 13b, 14, 15 (all), 16, 17t, 18bl, 19tr; Shutterstock: 2/3bg, 11r, 24bg;
Subaru Observatory: 21b; ticktock picture archive: 5tr, 6/7bg, 10/11bg, 10bl, 10br, 13t, 14/15bg, 17b, 18br, 18/19bg, 21t,
22/23bg
Every effort has been made to trace the copyright holders, and we apologise in advance for any unintentional omissions.
We would be pleased to insert the appropriate acknowledgements in any subsequent edition of this publication.

Contents

Where is Pluto?

Pluto is part of the **solar system**. Like the eight planets, it travels around the Sun. Pluto is a **dwarf planet**.

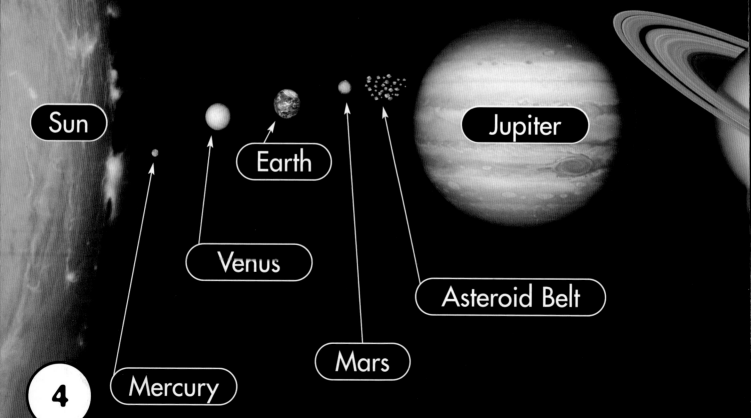

Sun

Mercury

Venus

Earth

Mars

Asteroid Belt

Jupiter

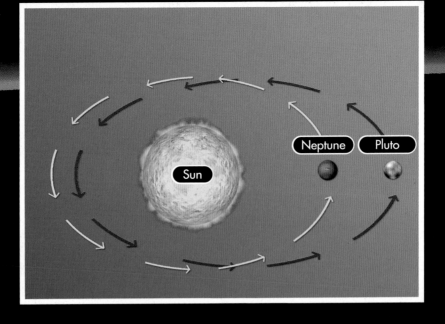

Pluto travels around the Sun once every 249 **Earth years**. This journey is called its **orbit**. The time it takes for a planet to travel around the Sun once is called a **year**. Sometimes Pluto is closer to the Sun than Neptune.

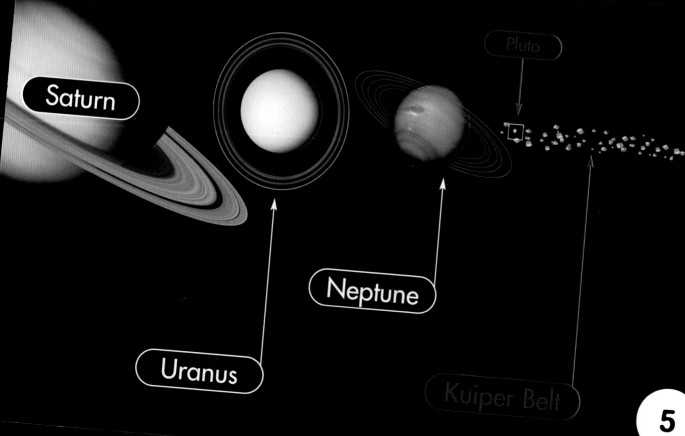

Saturn

Uranus

Neptune

Pluto

Kuiper Belt

The Outer Solar System

Before **astronomers** first discovered Pluto, most people thought they had found everything that travelled around the Sun.

Pluto

Saturn

Uranus

Neptune

Kuiper Belt

Now we know that there are many more objects far out in the **solar system**. This group of objects is called the Kuiper Belt.

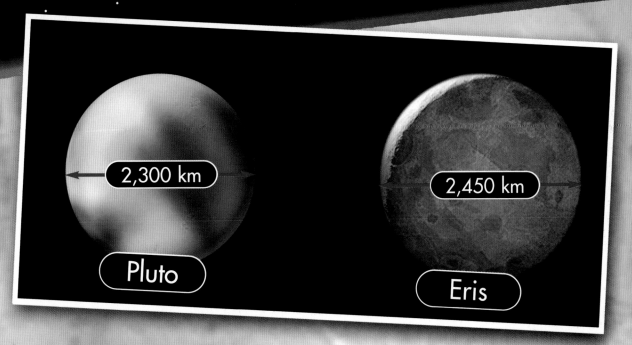

2,300 km

Pluto

2,450 km

Eris

The **dwarf planet** Eris was discovered in 2005. It is bigger than Pluto.

Kuiper Belt

No-one knows how many more dwarf planets are waiting to be discovered.

Pluto: A Dwarf Planet

Pluto is only about 2,300 kilometres across. It is smaller than some of the **solar system's** moons, including our own Moon.

5,594 km

Earth's Moon

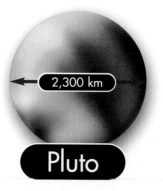

2,300 km

Pluto

In 2006, **astronomers** decided that Pluto is too small to be called a planet. It is to be called a **dwarf planet** instead.

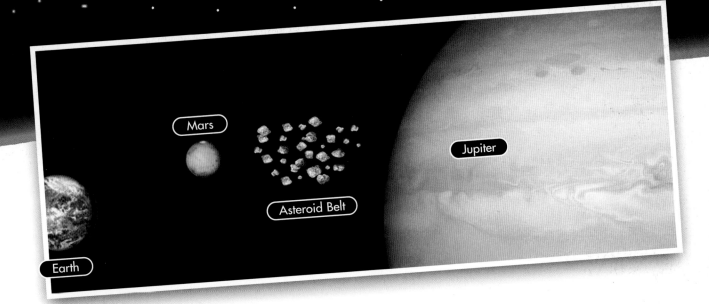

Mars

Asteroid Belt

Jupiter

Earth

Most dwarf planets, like Pluto and Eris, are in the Kuiper Belt, which lies beyond Neptune. There is one dwarf planet in the **Asteroid** Belt between Mars and Jupiter.

Ceres

This is Ceres, which is about 1000 kilometres across.

Dwarf Planet Facts

We know **very little** about what it is like on Pluto and the other distant **dwarf planets.** No space mission has reached them, and they are too small or too far away to see any details using telescopes.

This is a photograph of Pluto through a very strong telescope.

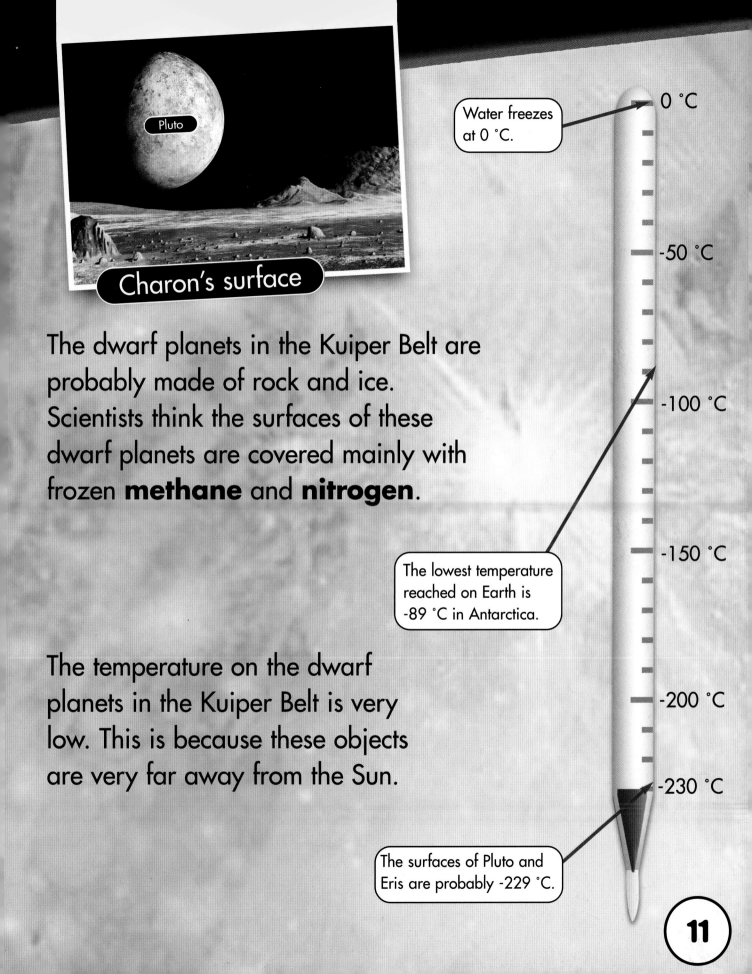

Pluto

Charon's surface

The dwarf planets in the Kuiper Belt are probably made of rock and ice. Scientists think the surfaces of these dwarf planets are covered mainly with frozen **methane** and **nitrogen**.

The temperature on the dwarf planets in the Kuiper Belt is very low. This is because these objects are very far away from the Sun.

Water freezes at 0 °C.

The lowest temperature reached on Earth is -89 °C in Antarctica.

The surfaces of Pluto and Eris are probably -229 °C.

0 °C

-50 °C

-100 °C

-150 °C

-200 °C

-230 °C

The **orbit** of Pluto and Eris sometimes takes them closer to the Sun. When this happens, the surface changes.

atmosphere

Pluto

Sunlight changes some of the frozen surface of Pluto and Eris into a gas, giving them a thicker **atmosphere**.

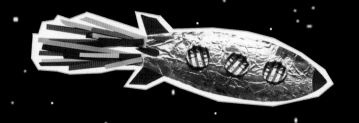

As Pluto and Eris move further away from the Sun, the atmosphere gets colder. This means that the gasses turn solid again and fall to the ground.

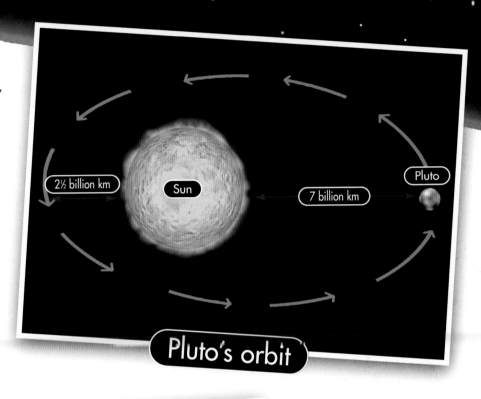

2½ billion km

Sun

7 billion km

Pluto

Pluto's orbit

Charon

Pluto's surface

This means that Pluto and Eris have a kind of snow, a bit like Earth!

13

Pluto's Moons

Pluto's main moon is called Charon (pronounced kai–ron). Charon is almost half the size of Pluto itself. Charon wasn't discovered until 1978.

Charon

Pluto

Some **astronomers** say that Charon is not Pluto's moon. They say that Charon is also a **dwarf planet**. Charon might have been made when a giant object hit Pluto millions of years ago.

Charon

Pluto

Pluto

Charon's surface

Charon is very different from Pluto. The surface has a lot of frozen water on it.

The Kuiper Belt

The Kuiper Belt is a great mass of objects, large and small. These objects all **orbit** around the Sun.

Kuiper Belt

There are hundreds more objects in the Kuiper Belt than there are in the **Asteroid** Belt. They are made mainly of ice. Most of them are quite small.

Some **astronomers** say that at the very edge of the **solar system** there is something called the Oort cloud.

This is a painting of what the Oort cloud could look like.

Oort Cloud

Halley's comet

Scientists think that **comets** come from the Oort cloud.

Pluto in History

Pluto was discovered in 1930. The American **astronomer** Percival Lowell had worked out in the 1890s that there was a large object further out than Neptune. He called it Planet X.

Percival Lowell Observatory

Percival Lowell

The hunt for the new planet took place in the Percival Lowell **Observatory** in Arizona, USA.

At last, in January 1930, the American astronomer Clyde Tombaugh discovered Pluto.

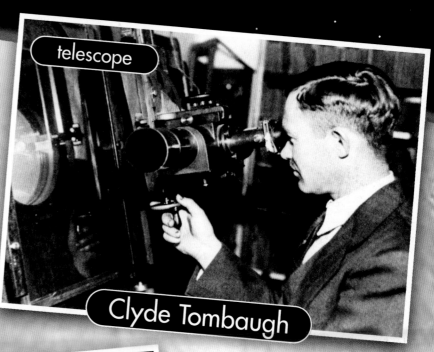

telescope

Clyde Tombaugh

Pluto

Pluto was named after the Roman God of the Underworld.

What Can We See?

We don't know much about the Kuiper Belt objects. They are too far away from Earth to take clear photographs.

This is a photograph of Pluto and Charon. It is one of the clearest images we have so far. It was taken by the **Hubble Space Telescope**.

This is the Subaru **Observatory** in Hawaii. It has been studying Pluto and the Kuiper Belt objects to help the New Horizons mission.

Subaru Observatory

Pluto

Charon

This is a photograph from the Subaru Observatory. It shows Pluto and Charon.

The New Horizons Mission

On 19th of January 2006, the New Horizons **space probe** was launched. Its mission is to explore Pluto, Charon and the Kuiper Belt.

This is a photograph of the New Horizons rocket being launched.

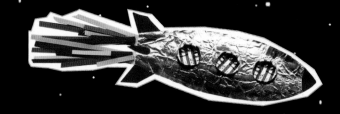

The space probe will reach Jupiter by March 2007. It should reach Pluto in 2015. Between 2016 and 2020, it will study objects in the Kuiper Belt.

space probe

Charon

Pluto

Kuiper Belt

space probe

These are paintings of the New Horizons space probe above Pluto, and by the Kuiper Belt.

There is still a lot to learn about the **solar system** we live in.

Glossary

Asteroid A rocky object that orbits the Sun. Most asteroids orbit the Sun between Mars and Jupiter.

Astronomers People who study space, often using telescopes.

Atmosphere The gases that surround a star, planet or moon.

Comets Objects usually made of ice and frozen gas that are in orbit around the Sun.

Dwarf planet An object smaller than a planet that orbits around the Sun.

Earth years A year is the time it takes for a planet to orbit the Sun. An Earth year is 365 days long.

Hubble Space Telescope A telescope that orbits the Earth. Its pictures of space are very clear because it is outside of Earth's atmosphere.

Methane A colourless gas with no smell. It burns easily.

Nitrogen A colourless gas with no smell. It can be found in the Earth's atmosphere and all living things.

Observatory A building that has huge telescopes and tools to study space.

Orbit The path that a planet or other object takes around the Sun, or a satellite takes around a planet.

Solar system The Sun and everything that is in orbit around it.

Space probe A spacecraft sent from Earth to explore the solar system. It can collect samples and take pictures.

Year The time it takes a planet to orbit the Sun once.

Index